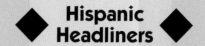

◆ **Hispanic Headliners** ◆

Selena Gomez

Actress and Singer

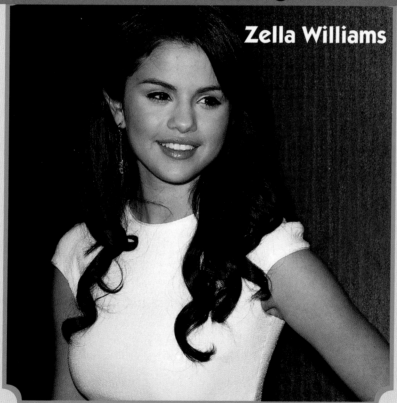

Zella Williams

PowerKiDS press™

New York

Published in 2011 by The Rosen Publishing Group, Inc.
29 East 21st Street, New York, NY 10010

First Edition

Editor: Joanne Randolph
Book Design: Kate Laczynski
Photo Researcher: Jessica Gerweck

Photo Credits: Cover, pp. 1, 13 (top) Jason LaVeris/FilmMagic/Getty Images; pp. 4, 5 Theo Wargo/ Wirelmage/Getty Images; pp. 6, 10 Jon Kopaloff/FilmMagic/Getty Images; p. 7 Michael Tran/ FilmMagic/Getty Images; pp. 9, 20 Mathew Imaging/WireImage/Getty Images; p. 11 Mark Perlstein/ Time & Life Pictures/Getty Images; pp. 12, 13 (bottom) Frederick M. Brown/Getty Images; p. 14 Todd Williamson/Wirelmage/Getty Images; p. 15 George Pimentel/Wirelmage/Getty Images; p. 16 Ray Tamarra/Getty Images; p. 17 Kevin Winter/Getty Images; p. 18 Mark Sullivan/Wirelmage/Getty Images; p. 19 Brian Ach/Wirelmage/Getty Images; p. 21 (top) Robert Benson/Getty Images; p. 21 (bottom) John Shearer/Wirelmage/Getty Images; p. 22 Jesse Grant/Wirelmage/Getty Images.

Library of Congress Cataloging-in-Publication Data

Williams, Zella.
  Selena Gomez : actress and singer / Zella Williams.
    p. cm. — (Hispanic headliners)
  Includes index.   4385 8603 11/10
  ISBN 978-1-4488-1458-9 (library binding) — ISBN 978-1-4488-1482-4 (pbk.) —
ISBN 978-1-4488-1483-1 (6-pack)
  1. Gomez, Selena, 1992—Juvenile literature. 2. Actors—United States—Biography—Juvenile literature.
3. Singers—United States—Biography—Juvenile literature. I. Title.
  PN2287.G585W55 2011
  791.4302'8092—dc22
  [B]
                                    2010005306

Manufactured in the United States of America
CPSIA Compliance Information: Batch #WS10PK: For Further Information contact Rosen Publishing, New York, New York at 1-800-237-9932

CONTENTS

Have you ever heard of Selena Gomez? If you have seen her work, then maybe you are a fan. She has played lots of parts on TV and in movies. She is best known for her work on *Wizards of Waverly*

Selena Gomez knew she wanted to become an actress at a young age.

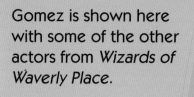

Place. She also sings in a band. She is just getting started, though. You may have heard some of her songs on the radio. If you have not heard of her yet, then you will!

Selena Gomez was born on July 22, 1992, to Mandy Cornett and Ricardo Gomez. She was born in New York City. Soon her family moved to Grand Prairie, Texas, though. This

Selena's father, Ricardo Gomez, has family in Guadalajara, Jalisco, Mexico.

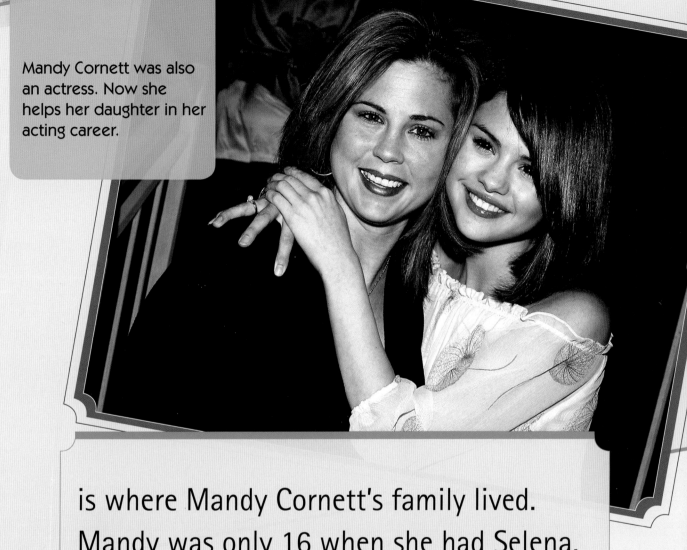

Mandy Cornett was also an actress. Now she helps her daughter in her acting career.

is where Mandy Cornett's family lived. Mandy was only 16 when she had Selena. They did not have a lot of money during that time.

Selena Gomez's parents **divorced** in 1997, when Selena was five. Her mother was an actress in the theater. Selena often went with her mother to **rehearsals**. It was during this time

Gomez's mother married Brian Teefy, who became Gomez's stepfather, in 2006.

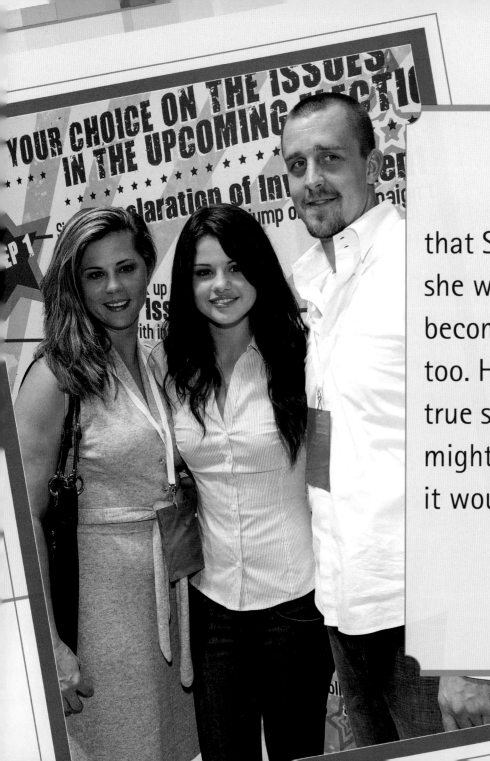

that Selena decided she would like to become an actress, too. Her wish came true sooner than she might have thought it would.

When Selena turned seven, she got a **role** as Gianna on *Barney & Friends*. She appeared in this role many times. The shows did not air until she was in fifth

Once Gomez got the part as Gianna, she started getting more parts.

Barney & Friends, the show on which Gomez got her start, has been on the air since 1992.

grade, though. Over the next few years, she got more small parts. One of these parts was in *SpyKids 3-D: Game Over*, in 2003.

In 2004, Selena Gomez started getting small parts on shows on the Disney Channel. She was in *The Suite Life of Zach & Cody* and *Hannah*

In 2009, *Wizards of Waverly Place* won an Emmy Award.

One of Gomez's costars on *Wizards of Waverly Place* is Jake T. Austin, shown with her here.

Montana. Then, in 2007, Selena landed her own show. She took a part as Alex Russo on *Wizards of Waverly Place.* In this show, Alex and her brothers are learning to use their magical powers.

The actors on *Wizards of Waverly Place* are giving a talk about their show here.

In 2008, Selena Gomez took a part in *Another Cinderella Story*. She also had movie roles in *Princess Protection Program* and *Wizards of Waverly Place: The Movie*. In 2009, she got a part in *Ramona and Beezus*,

Gomez and her friend Taylor Swift stand outside the first showing of *Another Cinderella Story*.

Demi Lovato (left) starred in *Princess Protection Program* with Gomez.

based on a book by Beverly Cleary. She has done some voice acting for movies, too, including *Horton Hears a Who!*

Selena Gomez does more than act. She also sings and dances. In 2008, she started a band called Selena Gomez & the Scene. The band's first album came out in September 2009. It is called *Kiss & Tell*.

Gomez sang a song from her first album on a TV talk show called *Good Morning America*.

Here Selena Gomez & the Scene play in Las Vegas on New Year's Eve 2009.

It sold 66,000 copies in the first week! Gomez has also recorded songs for some movie sound tracks. Some of these were for movies she had a part in but some were not.

Selena Gomez also does a lot of **charity** work. She helped in the UR Votes Count **campaign** in 2008. This campaign tried to get young people to learn more

A young girl gave Gomez this card at a UR Votes Count event.

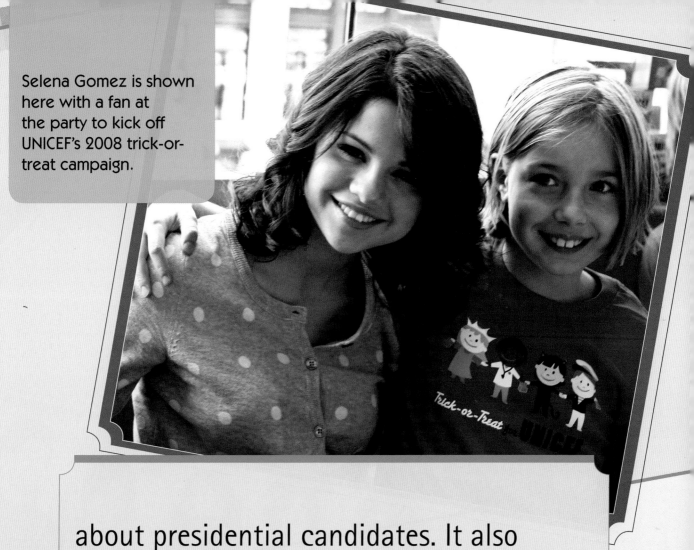

Selena Gomez is shown here with a fan at the party to kick off UNICEF's 2008 trick-or-treat campaign.

about presidential candidates. It also encouraged them to vote. She was named one of UNICEF's goodwill **ambassadors** in 2009.

Selena Gomez has been **nominated** for and won many awards for her work. She won a Kid's Choice Award in 2009 for *Wizards of Waverly Place*.

Here the actors from *Wizards of Waverly Place* show off their Emmy Awards.

Selena Gomez is shown here thanking people for her 2009 Alma Award.

She won some Teen Choice Awards that year, too. She has also been nominated for Alma and Imagen awards for her work as a Latina artist.

Here Gomez receives her 2009 Teen Choice Award.

We are sure to see a lot more from Selena Gomez. She already has her own production company, called July Moon Productions. She also has a clothing line,

called Dream Out Loud by Selena Gomez. What else will she do? The sky is the limit for this young actress and singer!

GLOSSARY

ambassadors (am-BA-suh-durz) People who are voices for countries or groups and who visit other countries or groups to share a message.

campaign (kam-PAYN) A plan to get a certain result, such as to win an election.

charity (CHER-uh-tee) A generous act.

divorced (dih-VORST) Ended a marriage.

nominated (NO-muh-nayt-ed) Picked to do a certain job.

rehearsals (rih-HER-sulz) Practices for something, such as a play.

role (ROHL) A part played by a person or thing.

INDEX

WEB SITES

Due to the changing nature of Internet links, PowerKids Press has developed an online list of Web sites related to the subject of this book. This site is updated regularly. Please use this link to access the list:
www.powerkidslinks.com/hh/gomez/